inner-lude

inner-lude

aliyah branay

*for those
ready to
dive into
their inner
beings*

there were smiles, laughter, and tears to bring forth these words. these pages lie my heart, truths, dreams, and some of the most teaching years of my life.

-i n n e r -l u d e

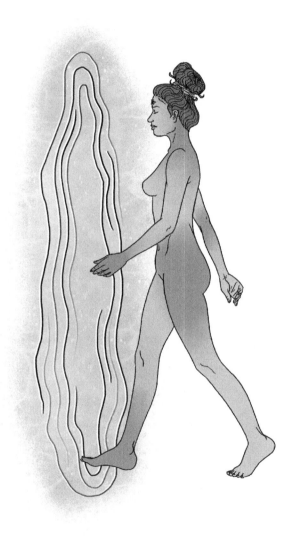

love like hip hop

i love you like i love hip hop.
in the most deep and intimate ways.
you settle and spark flames
within my brain.
etched and engraved
within every part of my being.
remnants of you always remain.
you bring me happiness,
joy and pain.
you leave me in my feelings
on most days,
and see into my soul
in the most intimate ways.
you connect, reach, and pull
for me when i am distant.
our union aids my healing
and i know for you,
it is the same.
it's like we need each other.
breathe each other.
feed each other.
through mental and
spiritual realms.
if you're meant to be mine
only time will tell.
you have been there on my
darkest days.

you have pulled me
through the rain.
through you i find passion
and your words ignite my change.
with you i have grown from a kid
to the woman i am today.
we connect through words
and vibrations,
we are one in the same.
without you my life would
not be the same.
i can't help but to love you
like i love hip hop.

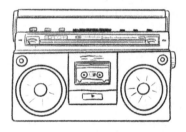

i want
the kind
of love
he writes
about in
his poetry.

r e a l,

v u l n e r a b l e ,

h o n e s t,

r a w.

as these words gather
upon the pages,
so does my peace
and the settling of my soul

you give me purpose,
you give me life

-pens, rhymes, and pages

you remind me of an
isley brother's song

a soulful,
smooth,
soothing,
classic,

a melodic,
irresistible,
rhythm

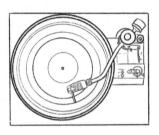

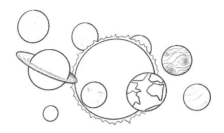

these words dance
and dance around
in my head,
flow into my heart
and out through
the ink filled
remnants of my
beating soul.
this pretty poetry
spilling and flowing
onto to this leaf like
its meant to be,
like its ordained by
something or someone
i cannot see.

-divine order?

the feel and sound of
your vibrations soothe me,
your music gives me clarity,
your hue brings me peace
and leaves me with newfound wisdom.
you fill me with the patience i seem to lose,
and every time you reach the shore,
pieces of me are reborn.
within you,
i find me.

-*ocean therapy/beach bum anonymous*

it's a weird thing to be a writer. having all these
thoughts constantly swimming round' and
round' in your head. staring off into space.
exposing your deepest secrets. zoning out of
many conversations only to talk day and night
with your pen and paper.

i close my eyes as Luther Vandross plays.
his music keeps me sane,
keeps me from
folding into the pain,
when i hear his voice
i know everything will be okay

-dancing with Luther

i flow this pen
like i'm writing verses
like somehow i'm
kendrick or jermaine
like somehow they will
know my name
or somehow these
words will pave my way

falling in love
with yourself
is one of
the most beautiful
things to ever experience

you will always
matter in my eyes

-*you are worth so much more than you know*

i don't mind being alone
when i have found peace
within me

and freed myself of
my own and others
toxic energies

you mean the world to me
but if you do not love me
i will not stay

i won't let what happened
between us destroy me

-unbreakable

you remind me of
the perfect rhyme,
the kind that makes
you pause the track
and press rewind

love is unconditional,
so i will not bash you
or use your name in vein.
i will love you from afar
like i have always loved you.
silently,
q u i e t l y,
without ever touching you
or receiving your heart.

-a quiet,
empty spark

i was never acting with
my feelings for you,
it always felt like loving you
was my destiny

it's not what happens that defines us,
it's how we respond

you are strong enough
to leave them behind

i wish for the right words
to describe us.
to describe you
and the rush you
leave within me.
you have been
by far the hardest muse
to free from my spirit.
yet, i still walk away
and close the door on us
just like you have done
so many times before.
the only difference is
this is no swinging door.
the door i've closed is shut.
there is no longer room for ins and outs.

-the last time you walked away,
you decided for the both of us

you leave me
confused,
dazed,
in limbo,
constantly wondering if
we are moving forward
or backward,
constantly trying to
understand what we are,
your intentions,
and do they lie any
further than the sheets
in your bedroom

messages from you are
the best ones

i try to learn you,
discover you,
dive deeper
into our connection
that we've been trying
upon for years,
but you don't want to share.
you keep your heart sealed
and your past secret.
everything secret.
everything sealed.
you won't let me through
and i try not to take it personally
but,
how do we move forward?
how do we grow together?
without sharing
o u r s e l v e s?
i am exhausted
of trying.
i no longer know
any more ways
to get through,
i can no longer keep
doing this shit
with you.
i can only define
this as your way
of telling me
you don't

see more in me,
you don't trust me,
you don't feel like you
can be free with me,
you don't want to grow
this situation,
and i can't keep trying
to convince you.
now you have convinced me
that this connection
was an illusion
and you,
i will not keep pursuing.

-*t i r e d*

the people you love
may not love you.
but don't let that
change your loving
ways.
keep your heart pure
and loving.

-this world needs more love

we make love with our eyes,
words,
lips,
and then our souls.
even without speaking
a single word,
we travel to the unknown.
exploring love in its
infinite forms.
expressing,
connecting,
professing,
both internally,
and externally.
verbally
and then silently.
it's like you're inside
of me,
like you reside
in me,
yet we speak
no words.
there is no need.
we are in sync
through telepathic keys,
that magnetize you
and me.
i love you infinitely

i can give you my trust,

but my intuition will
over power my desire
to believe the words
you so beautifully
paint

-in-tune

i knew you would call
i tried to warn you that
it would be hard
to get through
but you are so stuck
in your ways
you couldn't fathom
that things could
change

you bring out
parts of me
that i don't expose,

you make me
feel like its okay
to be free

you leave me on a
gravitational pull
that i can't escape.
within my soul,
you lie in
a sacred place,
you make me forget
the pain,
you give me hope
for better days.

-*men like you are rare*

there is so much strength
in being comfortable
with being alone,
you no longer need others
to fill personal voids,
you stand tall and strong
all on your own

i can't catch you
in any moment
other than when
the beat plays

when we sex

we connect

like we are in love

but we don't dare

speak those words

we remain on this cycle,

dibbling and dabbling,
loving and leaving,
communicating and
then disappearing,
i cannot take it,
i want better
and that means
leaving you behind
despite my feelings

-i didn't stop loving you,
i started loving myself

some things are
not meant to be
and it is okay
to walk away

-your blessings are coming

open your heart
to the endless
possibilities
that there are
good things coming
your way

the most beautiful people
are the ones that are
unafraid to be themselves

sometimes we may find ourselves
standing alone so that we remain
true to our values, morals,
and higher selves

what do we gain by
inflicting the same
pain that has been
inflicted upon us,

onto others?

being happy
and unbothered
is success to me

we become so hooked
on finding love
that we forget to first
find ourselves

i wanted to un-peel
the layers of you
to discover your heart,
soul, and truth.
i wanted to become
one with your mind
and show you how
wonderful it was
to have you as mine.

i sit and think about you
wishing somehow the cards
would have fell differently,

wishing somehow we could
have communicated
and wishing somehow we
were honest

i am in the stages of self love
and healing

finding peace in my solitude,
strength in my individuality,
value in my being

what was once broken
is becoming repaired,

my heart,
mind and spirit

-*spiritual transformation*

choosing to be greater
than my circumstances

i talk with my spirit,
asking it for guidance,
reaching out to the
universal light force,
becoming intertwined
within my divinity,
and each time i am
reminded that my
path is one of its own,
one where i often
walk alone
and i must find my way,
my truth,
and becoming whole before
i can think to lay bricks
of foundation with
another soul

*-there can be no relationship foundation when you
do not have an internal one of your own*

i loved you back when it wasn't okay
back when your eyes told me i was special
and your lips said you were vulnerable
and your hands and heart felt weaved into mine

we were young once,
full of hopes and dreams
where do they go?
how did we lose ourselves
within time?
how did we forget to
enjoy life?
to go after what made our
spirits feel alive?

we will make it through all the rain
through all the dark days
and everything that broke
our spirits and caused us pain

-purple rain

both lost in a time where
time is everything,
it has become
the most valuable currency.
we are unable to love each other enough
because we are wrapped up in ourselves,
deep into our shells.
we are trying to make and pave a way,
for not only ourselves,
but for others.
i guess there is no time to love.

-bag chasing

you are so beautiful that
i just can't comprehend
why you choose to loosely
share your energy.
for they do not deserve you.

like vultures,
they drain and eat you up
until theirs nothing left

never pouring back into you
only tearing you apart

why do you stay?

we have to make our time of value
and leave our mark in this paradise
with all that we say, think, and do

i think it's possible i loved you way back then. way back when white tee's and baggy jeans were in. way back when we were in a circle free style battlin'. way back when we'd never think to blur the lines of being lovers and friends.

understanding that
i am in pain
but never letting
the pain become me

you are the only person
that can change your situation

-*do what needs to be done*

i'll keep my heart open
if you can show me
you're not just lonely
and your words are worth
holding onto

your lies
linger in my mind
and always reveal
themselves each
and every time

take my kindness
and think you have
leverage,
never knowing that
was exactly what i
expected of you.
knowing that kind people
often go undervalued,
and many never realize
that the one that is really
losing is themselves.
cause' despite your
wickedness,
we still wish you well.
we are living in
a state of peace,
while others drown
in their own creation
of hell.

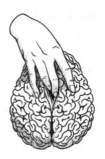

o p e n
my mind,

forget opening
my thighs

knowing that
sometimes
we are wrong
and learning
to admit that

you and i nod our heads
to the beats bumping
out of your stereo,
both in love with hiphop,
in love with the sound,
vibrations, and the lyrics,
in love with the feeling,
feeling the bass pump
through our souls,
this connection
tying our hearts

i am still human,
i am still making mistakes.
the difference is now i choose
to see the lessons in them
and learn to apply them.

understanding that
i will never
be perfect
but always working
towards achieving
my best

we can never
stop chasing
our passions,
we can never let
anything
stop us,
we must always
give it our all

you are strong enough
to face the doubters,
the non-supporters,
and the ones who cannot
seem to see your vision

be careful of letting
negative words
linger within your
mind

focusing on
growth,
transformation,
and complete self love

we lose many of
our loved ones
along the way,
it is for them that
we must keep going.

i wonder what you see
when our eyes meet

do you see my heart, soul,
and what i have potential
to be

or a woman whose flesh
you would like to slide
between

i do not need
to love anyone
for what they have,

for i have my own
and rather we come
together and grow

i think maybe many of us
have lost hope and choose
to use lovers instead
of exploring souls

i don't think
it's possible
to simmer
the flames
we left.
not after all the
love we made,
not after our
souls touched
in multiple ways,
and you left me
singing your name.

you are so intelligent,
i could ask you a sea of questions
and get swept away by the way
you think.
you are
brilliant,
genius,
b e a u t i f u l

our timing is
never right
and neither
are my words

at some point i dry the tears
and lift the blame i placed on others,

for it is my own shame to claim

i don't want revenge,
i just want peace
so you can leave freely
and i can get back to
loving me

g r o w t h.

i am no longer wanting the pain. and when
your name gets brought up, i no longer feel
ashamed. i learned to forgive myself for trusting
you more than i listened to my intuition, the
signals, and alarms. i am the light now and you
can't convince me that i should run back into
the dark.

we are all dreamers
told not to dream,
empty visions we toss
to the side,
convinced we cannot
live another life,
but that inner voice
whispers that it is all lies,
knowing that we should
move our feet and give it a try,
but the desire to be
secure screams louder
and leaves us terrified.
a tug of war that never ends…
but if we take a good look
at our ancestors,
we know it's in our destiny
to never succumb to fear,
but to always rise.

a lot of people are
influenced by you
and don't even know it

-keep grinding, keep shining

we are full of potential
that we often fail to act upon,
unaware that we could
change the world

if only we could
change our minds,
lift our feet,
and trust the pavement

beautiful,
melanin
beings.
aboriginally
born free,
born scientist,
prophets,
healers,
inventors,
kings and queens,
our family tree is the root,
the first grown seed.
yet they hate our beings
and we all ask for is justice and peace.

that phone call left me speechless
left me lost, dazed, and scheming
trying to make sense of my purpose and my
reasons
i guess this is goodbye and we've ended our
season

-i will not let you be the reason i stop succeeding

the pain only pushed me,
taught me,
groomed me,
and blossomed my strength.

-i will always rise

it was clear you were broken,
so was i
and with time,
our wounds became our demise
i'll still love you until the end of
life, space, and time,
yet, i don't care if our souls are tied,
i refuse to keep settling for these
toxic and repetitive,
cycles and strides

it isn't about you anymore. it's about me and
what i need and what we will never be. despite
our potential their are limits we can never
reach. now it's time to set ourselves free.

-freedom

i will never succumb to the hurt, i will always
write my way through it.

loving you taught me impermanence. that
nothing is certain, nothing is infinite. it taught
me to love with out attachment and to enjoy
every second, hour, minute.

i wish you would've
saw more in me than
want to be's and tryna be's.
i wish you saw my
strength and weight,
and put more faith in me.

you made me feel
like i could be myself
in multitude.

with you i was inter dimensional,
with them it's always 3D.
and i wonder if i'll ever meet another soul
who sees the world like you and me.

they taught us how to numb and kill our selves.
not how to ease the wounds or soothe the
aches. they gave us drugs and guns to convince
us that it could transform the pain.

-now it's time to change

the grind never ends,
i'll never retire,
not even when my souls drifts
to the astral plane,
not even when they look over
my grave,
not even when the blood dries in
my veins,
they will always know my name

-real poets never die

i know you'll regret it
on your words
you'll chew then choke
and the truth will be exposed
and you'll be back with
more words to propose
and heaven knows
i'm not coming back this time

i wanted to crumble
i wanted to break
i wanted to hide
but my purpose is bigger than
my emotions
i had no choice but to rise

i told you all of my pain
and all you did was repeat it

some people are not worth risking your peace
for. you have too much going on to lose yourself
in someone's opinion or negative energy. let
them think what they want. let them move how
they want.

-everything does not deserve a response or reaction

having a higher frequency does not mean that you're perfect or that you're always happy. you're still human. you still have emotions and are going to make mistakes. it just means you choose to rise above the bullshit more than you will ever give in to the low vibrations. it means that you are working towards being the best you at all times and refuse to let lower vibrations consume you.

-the choice will always and forever be yours

*want more from
aliyah branay?*

instagram: @aliyahbranay
twitter: @aliyahbranay
website: aliyahbranay.com
email: aliyahbranaymgmt@gmail.com

Made in the USA
Middletown, DE
19 August 2021

46458644R00066